Francis Frith's
Around
Royal Tunbridge Wells

Photographic Memories

Francis Frith's
Around
Royal Tunbridge Wells

Geoffrey Butler and Keith Hetherington

FRITH
BOOK Co

First published in the United Kingdom in 2002 by
Frith Book Company Ltd

Paperback Edition 2002
ISBN 1-85937-504-9

British Library Cataloguing in Publication Data

Francis Frith's Around Royal Tunbridge Wells
Geoffrey Butler and Keith Hetherington

Frith Book Company Ltd
Frith's Barn, Teffont,
Salisbury, Wiltshire SP3 5QP
Tel: +44 (0) 1722 716 376
Email: info@francisfrith.co.uk
www.francisfrith.co.uk

Printed and bound in Great Britain

Front Cover: The Pantiles c1955 T87010

Contents

Francis Frith: *Victorian Pioneer*

FRANCIS FRITH, Victorian founder of the world-famous photographic archive, was a complex and multi-talented man. A devout Quaker and a highly successful Victorian businessman, he was both philosophic by nature and pioneering in outlook.

By 1855 Francis Frith had already established a wholesale grocery business in Liverpool, and sold it for the astonishing sum of £200,000, which is the equivalent today of over £15,000,000. Now a multi-millionaire, he was able to indulge his passion for travel. As a child he had pored over travel books written by early explorers, and his fancy and imagination had been stirred by family holidays to the sublime mountain regions of Wales and Scotland. 'What a land of spirit-stirring and enriching scenes and places!' he had written. He was to return to these scenes of grandeur in later years to 'recapture the thousands of vivid and tender memories', but with a different purpose. Now in his thirties, and captivated by the new science of photography, Frith set out on a series of pioneering journeys to the Nile regions that occupied him from 1856 until 1860.

Intrigue and Adventure

He took with him on his travels a specially-designed wicker carriage that acted as both dark-room and sleeping chamber. These far-flung journeys were packed with intrigue and adventure. In his life story, written when he was sixty-three, Frith tells of being held captive by bandits, and of fighting 'an awful midnight battle to the very point of surrender with a deadly pack of hungry, wild dogs'. Sporting flowing Arab costume, Frith arrived at Akaba by camel seventy years before Lawrence, where he encountered 'desert princes and rival sheikhs, blazing with jewel-hilted swords'.

During these extraordinary adventures he was assiduously exploring the desert regions bordering the Nile and patiently recording the antiquities and peoples with his camera. He was the first photographer to venture beyond the sixth cataract. Africa was still the mysterious 'Dark Continent', and Stanley and Livingstone's historic meeting was a decade into the future. The conditions for picture taking confound belief. He laboured for hours in his wicker dark-room in the sweltering heat of the desert, while the volatile chemicals fizzed dangerously in their trays. Often he was forced to work in remote tombs and caves where conditions were cooler. Back in London he exhibited his photographs and was 'rapturously cheered' by members of the Royal Society. His reputation as a

photographer was made overnight. An eminent modern historian has likened their impact on the population of the time to that on our own generation of the first photographs taken on the surface of the moon.

Venture of a Life-Time

Characteristically, Frith quickly spotted the opportunity to create a new business as a specialist publisher of photographs. He lived in an era of immense and sometimes violent change. For the poor in the early part of Victoria's reign work was a drudge and the hours long, and people had precious little free time to enjoy themselves. Most had no transport other than a cart or gig at their disposal, and had not travelled far beyond the boundaries of their own town or village. However,

by the 1870s, the railways had threaded their way across the country, and Bank Holidays and half-day Saturdays had been made obligatory by Act of Parliament. All of a sudden the ordinary working man and his family were able to enjoy days out and see a little more of the world.

With characteristic business acumen, Francis Frith foresaw that these new tourists would enjoy having souvenirs to commemorate their days out. In 1860 he married Mary Ann Rosling and set out with the intention of photographing every city, town and village in Britain. For the next thirty years he travelled the country by train and by pony and trap, producing fine photographs of seaside resorts and beauty spots that were keenly bought by millions of Victorians. These prints were painstakingly pasted into family albums and pored over during the dark nights of winter, rekindling precious memories of summer excursions.

The Rise of Frith & Co

Frith's studio was soon supplying retail shops all over the country. To meet the demand he gathered about him a small team of photographers, and published the work of independent artist-photographers of the calibre of Roger Fenton and Francis Bedford. In order to gain some understanding of the scale of Frith's business one only has to look at the catalogue issued by Frith & Co in 1886: it runs to some 670 pages, listing not only many thousands of views of the British Isles but also many photographs of most European countries, and China, Japan, the USA and Canada — note the sample page shown above from the hand-written *Frith & Co* ledgers detailing pictures taken. By 1890 Frith had created the greatest specialist photographic publishing company in the world,

Frith's death, a new card measuring 5.5 x 3.5 inches became the standard format, but it was not until 1902 that the divided back came into being, with address and message on one face and a full-size illustration on the other. *Frith & Co* were in the vanguard of postcard development, and Frith's sons Eustace and Cyril continued their father's monumental task, expanding the number of views offered to the public and recording more and more places in Britain, as the coasts and countryside were opened up to mass travel.

Francis Frith died in 1898 at his villa in Cannes, his great project still growing. The archive he created continued in business for another seventy years. By 1970 it contained over a third of a million pictures of 7,000 cities, towns and villages. The massive photographic record Frith has left to us stands as a living monument to a special and very remarkable man.

with over 2,000 outlets – more than the combined number that Boots and W H Smith have today! The picture on the right shows the *Frith & Co* display board at Ingleton in the Yorkshire Dales. Beautifully constructed with mahogany frame and gilt inserts, it could display up to a dozen local scenes.

Postcard Bonanza

The ever-popular holiday postcard we know today took many years to develop. In 1870 the Post Office issued the first plain cards, with a pre-printed stamp on one face. In 1894 they allowed other publishers' cards to be sent through the mail with an attached adhesive halfpenny stamp. Demand grew rapidly, and in 1895 a new size of postcard was permitted called the court card, but there was little room for illustration. In 1899, a year after

Frith's Archive: *A Unique Legacy*

FRANCIS FRITH'S legacy to us today is of immense significance and value, for the magnificent archive of evocative photographs he created provides a unique record of change in 7,000 cities, towns and villages throughout Britain over a century and more. Frith and his fellow studio photographers revisited locations many times down the years to update their views, compiling for us an enthralling and colourful pageant of British life and character.

We tend to think of Frith's sepia views of Britain as nostalgic, for most of us use them to conjure up memories of places in our own lives with which we have family associations. It often makes us forget that to Francis Frith they were records of daily life as it was actually being lived in the cities, towns and villages of his day. The Victorian age was one of great and often bewildering change for ordinary people, and though the pictures evoke an impression of slower times, life was as busy and hectic as it is today.

We are fortunate that Frith was a photographer of the people, dedicated to recording the minutiae of everyday life. For it is this sheer wealth of visual data, the painstaking chronicle of changes in dress, transport, street layouts, buildings, housing, engineering and landscape that captivates us so much today. His remarkable images offer us a powerful link with the past and with the lives of our ancestors.

Today's Technology

Computers have now made it possible for Frith's many thousands of images to be accessed almost instantly. In the Frith archive today, each photograph is carefully 'digitised' then stored on a CD Rom. Frith archivists can locate a single photograph amongst thousands within seconds. Views can be catalogued and sorted under a variety of categories of place and content to the immediate benefit of researchers.

Inexpensive reference prints can be created for them at the touch of a mouse button, and a wide range of books and other printed materials assembled and published for a wider, more general readership - in the next twelve months over a hundred Frith local history titles will be published! The day-to-day workings of the archive are very different from how they were in Francis Frith's time: imagine the herculean task of sorting through eleven tons of glass negatives as Frith had to do to locate a particular sequence of pictures! Yet

See Frith at www.francisfrith.co.uk

the archive still prides itself on maintaining the same high standards of excellence laid down by Francis Frith, including the painstaking cataloguing and indexing of every view.

It is curious to reflect on how the internet now allows researchers in America and elsewhere greater instant access to the archive than Frith himself ever enjoyed. Many thousands of individual views can be called up on screen within seconds on one of the Frith internet sites, enabling people living continents away to revisit the streets of their ancestral home town, or view places in Britain where they have enjoyed holidays. Many overseas researchers welcome the chance to view special theme selections, such as transport, sports, costume and ancient monuments.

We are certain that Francis Frith would have heartily approved of these modern developments in imaging techniques, for he himself was always working at the very limits of Victorian photographic technology.

The Value of the Archive Today

Because of the benefits brought by the computer, Frith's images are increasingly studied by social historians, by researchers into genealogy and ancestory, by architects, town planners, and by teachers and schoolchildren involved in local history projects.

In addition, the archive offers every one of us an opportunity to examine the places where we and our families have lived and worked down the years. Highly successful in Frith's own era, the archive is now, a century and more on, entering a new phase of popularity.

The Past in Tune with the Future

Historians consider the Francis Frith Collection to be of prime national importance. It is the only archive of its kind remaining in private ownership and has been valued at a million pounds. However, this figure is now rapidly increasing as digital technology enables more and more people around the world to enjoy its benefits.

Francis Frith's archive is now housed in an historic timber barn in the beautiful village of Teffont in Wiltshire. Its founder would not recognize the archive office as it is today. In place of the many thousands of dusty boxes containing glass plate negatives and an all-pervading odour of photographic chemicals, there are now ranks of computer screens. He would be amazed to watch his images travelling round the world at unimaginable speeds through network and internet lines.

The archive's future is both bright and exciting. Francis Frith, with his unshakeable belief in making photographs available to the greatest number of people, would undoubtedly approve of what is being done today with his lifetime's work. His photographs, depicting our shared past, are now bringing pleasure and enlightenment to millions around the world a century and more after his death.

Around Royal Tunbridge Wells
An Introduction

The legend of Tunbridge Wells is intriguing. In 980 AD, St Dunstan was hard at work in his forge at Mayfield in Sussex. St. Dunstan was a very pious man, and he was constantly being tempted by the Devil. One day he was making a golden chalice when the Devil decided to tempt him, disguised as a comely young maiden. This did not fool St Dunstan: realising it was the Devil, he tweaked his nose with the red-hot tongs he was holding. The Devil gave a mighty roar, leapt in the air and landed on the Common at Tunbridge Wells. Spotting the Springs, he bathed his nose in the waters, giving them their metallic flavour; these are chalybeate

springs, which doctors recommended for their special healing properties.

The Common continued its peaceful ways until 1606. In that year, Lord North was staying with his friend Lord Abergavenny at Eridge Castle. Lord North was suffering from the many excesses typical of that age; he was out riding one day when he saw the Springs. Recognising their brown coloration from his experience of continental spas, he borrowed a wooden bowl from a Mrs Humphreys who lived in a cottage nearby and drank some of the water. He was so impressed with the taste that he filled a flask and took the

spring water to London for analysis. The results proved positive, and Lord North's health also improved. News soon spread, and visitors started arriving at the spring to take the waters.

In 1630 Charles I and his wife Queen Henrietta Maria, accompanied by his court, visited the Springs and were accommodated in tents on the Common. In 1632, a Doctor Rowzee of Ashford published a book which attributed wonderful healing properties to the waters. This caused an influx of visitors and in 1663 King Charles II and his wife Queen Catherine of Braganza arrived. Queen Catherine was suffering from infertility, a condition that Doctor Rowzee said could be cured by taking the waters. The Queen stayed a month, and it is recorded that during her stay she suffered from sickness. However, this sickness was not caused by pregnancy, but was due to the fact that the Queen did not like the water.

Mrs Humphreys, who lent Lord North a wooden bowl to taste the waters, became the first 'Dipper' at the Springs. She continued in this post until her death in 1678 aged 102 - surely a proof of the healing capacity of the waters.

In 1697 Princess Anne (later Queen Anne) came to the Walks accompanied by her son, the Duke of Gloucester. The Walks were very muddy, and the Duke slipped and fell in the mud. The Princess made a donation of £100 to the Council to pay for the paving of the Walks. When she returned the next year this had not been done and she left in disgust

never to return. In 1700 the Walks were paved with clay bricks that were baked in a pan to give them a uniform size. The paving tiles were called pantiles, and so the Walks were renamed. In 1678-1679 the chapel of King Charles the Martyr was built close to the Walks and thus became the chapel of the Walks. A school was established at the chapel, providing education for 50 or more poor boys and girls.

In 1682 the first buildings appeared on the Walks. These buildings were badly designed and not really in keeping with the area. A fire in 1687 destroyed most of the buildings, and more inspired planning and building followed; this resulted in the attractive colonnade that forms a major feature of the Pantiles today.

The Pantiles proved so popular that the visitors required more amusements than the healing springs alone could provide. Consequently, entertainment in the form of dancing, games and above all gambling soon became the established custom, and a Master of Ceremonies was appointed to organise the programme for the visitors. The most famous of these was Richard 'Beau' Nash, who came to the Pantiles in 1735; his reign continued until his death in 1762 aged 87. Beau Nash introduced a strict regime, and visitors were expected to follow this. They were also expected to contribute gratuities to the chapel, the Assembly Rooms, the waiters, the dippers and the sweepers.

If visitors also took part in the various games

of chance, a stay at the Pantiles could prove costly. Gambling became such an obsession that in 1730 and 1731 laws were passed banning all games except cards; this applied especially to games which involved numbers, such as roulette. The law was soon bypassed by an enterprising Tunbridge Wells resident who invented the E O Board, where the letters E (evens) and O (odds) were substituted for numbers. This proved highly popular, but most unprofitable for Nash, who became involved in lawsuits regarding monies due to him. He came out of this badly, and in 1748 all gaming but for cards was once again declared illegal. With the death of Beau Nash and the restrictions on gaming, the Pantiles passed its zenith.

The Pantiles continued to be graced with shops, coffee houses and inns, whilst the surrounding area, which was called the village, contained the lodging houses and the more ornate houses for the gentry. Trade was seasonal and ran from April till October.

Next to the Pantiles was a small stream, part of the network of streams that fed into the Medway. This stream had an important function: it divided Kent from Sussex. The building in the Pantiles area continued, with the Upper Walk containing the Spring, the music gallery and the shops, and the Lower Walk containing the inns and lodging houses. As the Lower Walk was developed, the stream was diverted into culverts and built over. This caused some difficulty, as many of the premises had parts in both Kent and Sussex. For instance, when Sarah Baker built her theatre in the Lower Walk in 1786, the auditorium was in Kent whilst the stage was in Sussex. This was an ideal situation for actors who owed debts to a county bailiff, as a few yards would take them into sanctuary. The county border was changed in 1934, and now the Kent/Sussex border meanders in and out of the many places near the town.

Another interesting question was the ownership of the Pantiles. This was claimed by the Manor of Rusthall, but the freeholders, led by the Earl of Abergavenny, instituted law proceedings in 1732. This resulted in the Manor Act of 1739, which divided the Pantiles into three parts: one part (buildings numbers 18 to 44) belonged to the freeholders, and the other two parts to the Manor. The freeholders were also entitled to one third of the revenue from the Common and rights of herbage.

In the other part of the town, religious enthusiasm continued to grow, aided by John Wesley, who paid several visits to the town in 1778 and 1784. The school at the chapel of King Charles the Martyr still flourished, and boys were admitted at six and girls at eight years old.

The town was still very popular with royalty. In 1822 the Duchess of Kent, accompanied by her daughter Princess Victoria (the future Queen Victoria), visited the town. Princess Victoria obviously liked her stay, as she revisited in 1826,

1827, 1834 and 1835. In 1834 she stayed at the Royal Sussex Hotel on the Lower Walk, and her visit was commemorated by the superb coat of arms of the Duke and Duchess of Kent which still stands over the main doorway.

Between 1828 and 1834, Decimus Burton and John Ward carried on a building programme which encompassed the Holy Trinity Church, shops and business premises in Calverley Road up to Calverley Park, the Crescent, and other buildings. This was followed by the opening of the first railway station in 1845, followed by a second station in 1866. This gave Tunbridge Wells easy access to London and the coast, which previously could only be reached by stage coach.

With the spread of the population, new churches were built, and most churches arranged for schools to be erected so that each parish had its own day and Sunday schools. There were numerous private schools, including Rose Hill school, which had Robert Baden Powell, defender of Mafeking and founder of the Scout movement, as a pupil.

On the Common, cricket was played by Kent in most seasons from 1840 to 1880. In 1882 an England team comprising many famous players, including W G Grace, played an Australian team and beat them.

What is now Showfields was the site of the Agricultural Show Grounds. It was here that Sir David Salomons, Mayor of Tunbridge Wells, held the very first motor show to be held in England. Sir David was a most enterprising man and a great innovator. He closed the show with a great flourish by driving his car - without the compulsory red flag - to the railway station, probably in excess of the legal speed limit of 4 miles per hour.

In 1870 the Great Hall was built, and many shows took place there. In 1902 the Opera House was built, and this attracted many of the famous performers of the day. The Opera House was so called not because it was the intention to hold performances of opera, but because a much-respected clergyman, Canon Hoare, considered the name 'theatre' to be unsuitable.

An important date for the town was April 1909, when King Edward VII granted the town the title of Royal Spa, thus giving it the right to style itself Royal Tunbridge Wells.

Between the wars the town grew rapidly. In 1934 the Kent and Sussex Hospital was built, which now badly needs to be replaced. A new Civic Centre was begun in 1937, the Assembly Hall and the police station opened in 1939, and the library, together with the museum and the art gallery, date from 1952. Within the museum there is a very large collection of Tunbridge ware, the form of marquetry for which the town is famous. Trinity Church was saved from demolition by an enthusiastic band of volunteers, and is now a very active theatre and art centre. In 1992 the Royal Victoria Shopping Centre opened, proving a great attraction for shoppers for

miles around.

In 1974 Tunbridge Wells became a District Council, embracing many rural areas including interesting and historic places such as Lamberhurst, Hawkhurst and Cranbrook amongst many others.

At the north end of the town, away from the main shopping centre, an industrial site has been developed. This is a fast-growing area. It includes not only light industrial premises, but also car, furniture, carpet and electrical warehouses, as well as many other trades. There are also large supermarkets here. Recently an extensive cinema project has been opened, and further development is planned.

Perhaps the town's greatest asset is its position in the centre of the Weald of Kent; from here there is easy access to many historic towns and villages, a few of which are illustrated in this book. In addition, the town is surrounded by the many orchards and farms that help to give the area the name 'the garden of England'. It is no wonder that so many people in Tunbridge Wells say that they will never leave it.

The Pantiles
London Road and Common

The Pantiles c1890 T87002
This view was taken from Linden Park Road. On the left, an ornate
lamp hangs next to the premises of F Featherstone, a baker who
retired from the bakery business in 1902. Next door was the shop
of R Pelton, a printer and stationer, who produced directories of
the town. To the right is the old Royal Victoria and Sussex hotel,
which was visited in 1834 by Princess Victoria; adjoining it is the
old Corn Exchange. The frontage of both these buildings was
retained during the redevelopment of the area in 1986.

The Pantiles c1955 T87059
The fine ceilings and mouldings compliment the pillars of the
colonnade outside the shop of Dust and Co. To the right is
the bandstand, which was built in 1900, then rebuilt in 1973.
To the left of the bandstand is the Old Gloster Tavern,
a timber-framed building which dates from 1700.

The Pantiles c1960 T87076
Here we see the Garden of Rest in the Pantiles, created in 1937 on the site of some houses that had fallen into disrepair. Many people were upset when in 1985 the owners of the site decided to build new shops with flats above on this site, with the loss of the garden.

The Pantiles c1955 T87087
The Garden of Rest is on the left of this photograph, and we can also see the colonnade which enabled visitors to shop under cover all down one side of the Pantiles. The clock advertising the Regency Restaurant was installed in 1924.

The Pantiles c1960 T87075

In the centre of this photograph is the church of King Charles the Martyr, which dates from 1676. On the right is the premises of Dust & Co, who took over the draper's business of R Corke in 1889. They had other properties on the Pantiles where they carried on the business of drapers, milliners, glovers, and art needlework. In 1942 they were taken over by Bobby and Co, but still traded under their own name until the late 1960s.

The Pantiles c1960 T87061
The white building straight ahead is the Chalybeate Spring,
discovered by Lord North in 1606. The gates lead to steps that go
down to the spring, where a dipper will serve the water to you. On
the left is the outfitters Fox Brothers, who were established in 1892
and only ceased trading in the last few years. To the right of the
spring is Boots the Chemist, whose stay on the Pantiles lasted from
1906 until 1987. The wine merchants on the right-hand side is
Prentis; it occupies a Grade II listed building which became a shop
in 1768. Today it trades as the Vintry.

The Pantiles c1890

T87001

We are looking back from Bath Square, with the General Post Office on the right. The position of postmaster of Tunbridge Wells was long held by the Nash family; first by John Nash in 1823, then by William Nash, who so built up the postal business that it outgrew its Pantiles site and a new post office had to be built in Vale Road in 1896. To the left of the post office is the chemist's shop of Alfred Nicholson, who had these new premises built here in 1884. The photograph offers a good insight into the dress and prams of the time, and note the bath chair.

The Pantiles c1910 T87001a
The delivery cart belonged to William Biggs, who had a grocery and general provisions shop at No 13 from 1870.
The clock is advertising the Cadena Café, who started their business on the Pantiles in 1902 and stayed until the
Regency restaurant took over. Note the street lamp at the top of the steps on the left-hand side.

The Pantiles c1955 T87009
On the railings above the premises of Dust & Co is a board stating 'Erected 1664'. This was the year that the manor of Rusthall began to develop that part of the Pantiles. On the left is R A Ashby's butcher's shop - his name is picked out in tiles at the front of the shop. He had two farms nearby where he bred pedigree white pigs. He died in 1955. Today the shop still bears his name, but is no longer a butcher's, but a picture gallery.

The Pantiles c1955 T87063
Compare this photograph with T87001 (pages 22-23). A flower bed has been added, and the ornate street lamp has been replaced by a very ordinary one. The post office has gone, to be replaced by Dust & Co, who sold soft furnishings and linen at this shop. The chemist has also gone. Note the pram parked by the spring.

The Old Fishmarket ▶
c1960 T87086
Dating from 1745, the Old Fishmarket served as a fish and poultry business under a Mr Hook, and later T Tolson and Macfisheries. When this photograph was taken, the premises were being used by J Ceci as an antiques shop. Mr Ceci came to the town in 1946 when he retired as clerk in charge of old prints at the British Museum. Today the premises operates as a tourist information centre.

▼ The Pantiles c1955 T87011
We are looking back along the Pantiles from the Chalybeate Spring. A notice on the first column told of the location of some of the original pantiles, which were baked clay tiles, used for paving in 1700; they have since been removed, and can be seen in the Tunbridge Wells museum. On the left is the Duke of York pub, now known as Chaplins, which became a pub in 1768. Note the sign for Gladys Wells, who sold corsets and lingerie: her business was taken over by Fox Brothers, who had been on the Pantiles since 1945.

The Pantiles c1955

T87010

We are looking from the spring toward Fishmarket Square, and we can see the shoe shop of Gertrude Philpot. The Philpot family had been in the shoe business for 150 years, and shoes were made on the premises. Gertrude Philpot died in 1956, and the business closed in 1970. Next door was the grocer J J Brooks & Son, who traded from the mid 1930s until the late 1960s. In the centre is an attractive brick building with an iron balcony: this was a florist and gardening shop run by the Charlton family.

London Road c1955

T87031

Looking up London Road from the Pantiles, we have the church of King Charles the Martyr to the right, followed by Lloyds Bank. When this photo was taken the traffic was light; today a roundabout, to help the flow of modern traffic, has replaced the lights shown here.

London Road 1875
T87006
The turreted building
in the centre of this
photograph is Vale
Tower, built in the
1830s as Romanoff
House, a school run
by Thomas Allfree - he
had been tutor to the
Russian royal family.
The other buildings
were demolished to
make way for hotels
such as the Vale Royal,
the Rosebank and the
Balmoral.

◄ **Mount Ephraim 1885**
T87004
The fine houses of
Mount Ephraim look
down on the lower
cricket ground and
common. To the right is
London Road, where
horses and carriages
wait; in later years
coaches would wait here.

◀ **A View from the Common c1955** T87012
The tall tower of Holy Trinity church dominates the area; designed by Decimus Burton, it was consecrated in 1829. In the centre are late Georgian and Regency houses. The bow-fronted house was Ashton Lodge, a former lodging house. Next to it, the house with the circular drive was used for many years as a surgery by Dr Selby-Green, Dr Hicks, and Dr Hawkes.

▼ **From Mount Ephraim c1870** 5390
Many of the town's older houses in London Road can be seen in this view from Mount Ephraim. The lack of trees on the common at the time was due to animals grazing - note the cow in the pond.

◀ **The Common c1885**
T87007
Here we see the lower cricket ground with railings around it. Many events have taken place on the pitch, including cricket, football, fairs, circuses and the Boxing Day meet of the local hunt.

◄ **Mount Pleasant c1955**
T87035
On the left we can see the row of shops known as Ritz Buildings, which came when the Ritz cinema was built in 1934. One shop was Strange Electrical, who had been founded in 1924 and still operate today, although the shop is now Heffle Electrical. At the moment the whole row of shops are under threat from redevelopment. In the centre of the photograph, the shop with the blinds down was Harridges Ltd, ladies' outfitters who were in business until the late 1950s.

Mount Pleasant and Town Centre

◀ **Mount Pleasant c1950** T87023
On the right with the blinds
down is the premises of
Mary Lee, who moved from the
High Street in 1936 to occupy
numbers 25 and 27 Mount
Pleasant. The shop employed
38 girls, and sought to rival the
fashion houses of London.
They tried to offer the best of
everything - the best designs,
the best materials, and the best
workmanship. In 1960 the firm
was associated with Bentalls of
Kingston.

◀ **Mount Pleasant c1955**
T87401
Looking down Mount
Pleasant toward the
Great Hall, we can see
the Cadena Tudor Café
on the left, which was
popular for its light lunches
and afternoon teas in the
conservatory. Next to it is
the chemist A E Hobbs,
which has been trading
under his name for over
100 years, even though
he died in 1938. On the
right-hand side are the
Ritz buildings and then the
car showroom of Rawsons,
which is today a Pizza Hut.

◀ **Church Road c1955**

T87019

We are looking towards Church Road from Crescent Road. The Ritz cinema was showing A J Cronin's 'The Green Years', starring Charles Coburn, Gladys Cooper, and Tom Drake. To the right is the tower of Holy Trinity church, which was consecrated in 1829; today it is an arts centre with a theatre and cinema.

◄ **The View from Mount Pleasant c1955** T87020
The Ritz cinema on the right was opened on 3 December 1934. The complex included 15 shops. The tall glass tower on the left was removed in the 1950s. Known during its life as the Ritz Essoldo, the Classic, the Cannon, the MGM and the ABC, the cinema was closed in 2000.

▼ **The Town Hall c1960**
T87078
Opened in March 1941, the Town Hall still causes controversy with local people; they would have preferred to have kept the Decimus Burton buildings, which were demolished to make way for this new development.

◄ **The War Memorial and the Library c1955** T87321
The library and museum are on the right; the library opened in 1952. A khaki-clad 'Tommy', a bronze statue by S Nicholson-Babb RBS, is the town's war memorial. It was unveiled on 11 February 1923 by Col Viscount Hardinge; the first wreath was laid by the mother of Captain Eric Dougall, a local man awarded the Victoria Cross posthumously for bravery at Messines, Belgium in 1918. The Opera House complex, behind the war memorial, incorporates Barclays Bank.

Crescent Road c1955 T87028

On the right, we can just see part of the Assembly Hall. Opened in 1939, it has housed many events such as dances, concerts, and shows, as well as other events. The ladies' outfitters Harridges Ltd can be seen opposite the Town Hall. The same scene today would be very different, as traffic often chokes up the roads here.

Mount Pleasant Road c1955 T87017

To the right is the Civic Centre and the library. The large domes are those of the Opera House, which opened in 1902 and served as a theatre and later as a cinema and a bingo hall; today it is a J D Wetherspoon pub. In March 1934 Louis Armstrong played at the Opera House. On the side of the bus is an advert for Timothy Whites & Taylors Ltd, who had premises in Calverley Road.

Grosvenor Road 1961 T87067
This area was known as the Five Ways, as traffic had five options of
where to travel. Today, with the closing off of Calverley Road, Lime
Hill Road and Mount Ephraim Road, perhaps it should be known as
Two Ways. The Times Tavern on the right-hand side was
demolished in 1984, and the chemist's was also demolished later.
On the left was the grocers Williamsons Ltd, later Tescos;
today it is a Costa Coffee House.

◀ **The Calverley Grounds c195**
T87018
The Calverley Grounds consist o
13 acres of land bought by the
corporation in 1920. A bandsta
was built in 1926 with a pavilior
but this was destroyed by a fire
bomb in 1940. The tea house w
also burnt down in recent years
but it has been rebuilt. Between
the trees the spire of St Peter's
church can be seen. Note the
ornate lamps, and the little hut
where bookings were taken for
the tennis courts and mini golf.
Garden plots take up the left-
hand side of the winding path;
this area was later grassed over.

Calverley Grounds

◀ **The Calverley Grounds c1960**
T87084
In the centre we see the Calverley Hotel, rebuilt by Decimus Burton in 1840. The Calverley Grounds were once part of the gardens of the hotel. Today the hotel trades as the Hotel DuVin.

◀ **The Calverley Grounds c1965** T87072
In the centre of the rose beds we can see the Burmese bell, which was left to the town by Col E Sladen, a former mayor of the borough. With the consent of the corporation the bell was retained at his home, Rusthall Beacon, during the lifetime of his widow; after her death the bell was delivered to Sir Robert Gower, executor to Col Sladen's will, who passed it on to the corporation. The bell had been left to Col Sladen by his father, who was Queen Victoria's representative in Burma.

◀ **The Earls Court Hotel c195**
T87042
This hotel was erected in 186
on the site of an earlier house
by the Honourable F G
Molyneux, and was named aft
his father, the Earl of Sefton.
Following the death of F G
Molyneux in 1886, the house
was let out in apartments. The
house was sold in 1901, and a
lot of money was invested to
turn it into a hotel; in 1904 it
opened with 100 bedrooms.
Later, an insurance company
bought the property and turne
it into offices. Plans are now
going ahead to turn it back int
apartments.

Hotels

The White Ladies Guest House c1965 T87093
The White Ladies Guest House was in Bishops Down, and was run by Mrs R Repard in the 1950s. Later it became the White Ladies Residential Hotel, run by Mr C P Fox and Mrs H M Fox.

The Mount Ephraim Hotel c1965 T87092
Built in 1834 on the site of what was known as the Hare and Hounds, it became one of the towns premier hotels and added Royal to its title. In the 1970s it changed its name to the Royal Wells Inn. Note the sign on the left that said that the hotel sold Worthington Beer on draught.

St John's Church c1955 T87049

St John's church dates from 1858, and is built of Kentish ragstone
with Bath stone dressings. The church had many wealthy
benefactors, such as the Byng family from Great Culverden.
When Mr Byng died in May 1897, his widow donated £100 to
the St John's church tower fund 'in memory of one who was
forty years by my side'. Later she took on the financial
responsibility for the completion of the tower. Among other
donations to the enrichment of the church were the splendid east
window, a clock for the tower, and a new organ. When Mrs Byng
died in April 1906, the church flag was flown at half mast.

The Wellington Hotel c1965 T87090

John Braby, a working jeweller, bought the Royal Kentish Hotel, and later exchanged this for Mr Peake's palatial mansion on Mount Ephraim. Mr Braby obtained permission to convert the mansion into a hotel which was opened in 1875, and was called the Wellington after the Duke of Wellington. The rooms were named after Wellington battles, and in the garden there were aviaries. A self-made man, and architect of his own fortune, John Braby died in 1896. The hotel he founded still operates today and despite being changed in the 1990s, it is now back to its original name.

The Spa Hotel c1955 T87051

Two East Kent coaches are bringing visitors to the Spa Hotel, once the home of Major Martin Yorke. It became a hotel in 1880, and has continued to attract visitors to stay, or to enjoy the many events that the hotel puts on.

◀ **The Spa Hotel c1955**
T87037
This photograph of the Spa post office, complete with stamp machine and wall post box, is a nice link with the past. Like many other small post offices in the last few years it was closed, and in this case became a hairdresser's.

The Spa Hotel c1955
T87036

The Spa Hotel was once known as the Bishops Down Spa Hydropathic Sanatorium; it opened in 1878 with Turkish baths and a full range of hydropathic treatments. At the outset it attracted aristocratic and distinguished guests, but its popularity lapsed and the building became a hotel.

The Golf Links from the Spa Hotel c1965   T87089

The golf course was opened in 1890, and was described in 1963 as 'one of the most picturesque in the district; although only a 9-hole course, the perfection of its greens and fairways offer everything a golfer requires'. It is 2364 yards in length, and bogey 67 for 18 holes.

Major York's Road c1965   T87101

At the top of Major York's Road, and fronting Langton Road, is the large building that was once a busy coaching inn known as the White Hart. Built in 1631, its life after the coaching era was as a tea house, then as a restaurant called Petronellas, and later The Alpine Rose. In the 1980s it was bought by a stockbroker and became a pub once again called the Brokers Arms.

◄ **The High Rocks c1870**
5406
Two miles from Tunbridge
Wells are the High Rocks,
another outcrop of
sandstone rock. Stone Age
man is known to have used
the area, as the overhang of
the rocks offered good
shelter, and excavations in
1957 and 1958 showed that
there had been Iron Age
forts on the site. The rocks
became a tourist attraction
as early as 1670, when the
Duke of York (afterwards
James I) visited the area and
brought them to the
attention of the gentry.

Sandstone Outcrops

◀ **The Toad Rock c1870** 5404
One of the most visited sights in the Tunbridge Wells area is the sandstone outcrop of rocks at Denny Bottom, Rusthall. The large stone, resembling a toad, overlooks the 16th-century inn known as the Toad Rock Retreat. In March 1998 the inn was gutted by fire, but at a cost of £320,000 was rebuilt. Locals helped by supplying old photographs of the inn so that the new building could be as like the old inn as possible.

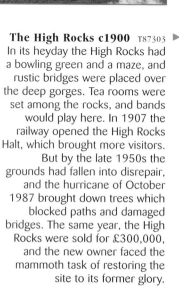

The High Rocks c1900 T87303 ▶
In its heyday the High Rocks had a bowling green and a maze, and rustic bridges were placed over the deep gorges. Tea rooms were set among the rocks, and bands would play here. In 1907 the railway opened the High Rocks Halt, which brought more visitors. But by the late 1950s the grounds had fallen into disrepair, and the hurricane of October 1987 brought down trees which blocked paths and damaged bridges. The same year, the High Rocks were sold for £300,000, and the new owner faced the mammoth task of restoring the site to its former glory.

The Wellington Rocks c1965 T87110
There can hardly be a child in the town who has not played on the
Wellington Rocks. They are named after the nearby Wellington
Hotel, although earlier they were called High Rocks, Mount Ephraim
Rocks and Castle Rocks.

Aerial View of Town

An Aerial View c1955 T87053
In the centre of this aerial photograph is an area known as
Harvey Town, after a previous owner of the land. In the late
1950s all this area was cleared to build a multi-storey car park.
Behind the library, which is the building to the left of the Town
Hall, stands the tall Technical Institute, which opened in 1902.
Next to it was the Monson Swimming Baths, which opened in
1898; they were closed in the late 1970s, and later demolished.

An Aerial View c1955 T87052

The open space at the top of the photograph is the Calverley Grounds. In the centre we can see the Town Hall complex, and the Opera House is next door. The building with the blinds down was Waymarks store, later Chiesman Ltd. This whole building was demolished and then rebuilt in 1988 to look exactly the same. Some alterations and demolition took place on the buildings on the left owing to the building of the Royal Victoria Place Shopping Centre, which opened in 1992.

Southborough and Bidborough

Southborough
St Peter's Church 1896 37900
Consecrated in August 1830, St Peter's church is built in brick and stone; it consists
of chancel, nave, north and south porches, and an eastern tower with a spire containing
a clock and six bells. There are several stained glass windows. Standing close to
Southborough cricket pitch, the church held a cricketers' service in 1951. Test cricketers
such as Frank Woolley, Colin Cowdrey, and the Rev David Sheppard attended.

Southborough
London Road 1900 44920
London Road is much busier today. Note the milk cart with churn standing by the lamp
post on the right. On the left-hand side is the shop of W Cushen, silk mercer and
undertaker; next is G Mercer, a greengrocer, then J Fielder, a stationer. The gabled
building with a covered balcony was the hairdresser F W Wiles, the watchmaker F Piper
and the fishmonger and poulterer C Hall. Further on were G Grantham & Sons,
bootmakers, A Brown, a builder and undertaker, E Ashdown, a confectioner,
F Simmonds, a tailor, and the Crown Inn.

Southborough, London Road c1955 S152004

It is fifty years after photograph 44920 (previous page). We are looking toward Tonbridge. A window cleaner with his barrow is busy cleaning the windows of Mrs Broomfield's ladies' hairdressing establishment. The shop on the right was the bakery of A Langford; the windows advertise Hovis, Darren and Vitbe bread. A blind shades the fishmonger's shop of H Robertson, and further on is G Green, the chemist. A lorry is parked outside the Imperial Hotel.

Southborough, London Road 1896 37888

Approaching Southborough from Tonbridge, on the right-hand side we have J Martin, the carrier, with a lamp outside; next to him is the butcher's shop of F Hackett, then T Edenborough, a harness maker. The Wesleyan Chapel, erected in 1870, was demolished when a new Methodist church was built further along the road in 1936. On the left is the Imperial Hotel at the junction with Pennington Road.

Southborough
London Road c1955 S152005
This is the same scene as 37888 (previous page) fifty-odd years later. The offices of J Martin are still there, though the lamp has gone. S White is running the butcher's shop, and next to him is the tea rooms of the Misses Sayers. V Still & Son, builders, occupy the other property, and the Wesleyan Chapel has gone. On the left is the Imperial Hotel. In May 1901 Caleb Cooper was granted a temporary licence to run the hotel, with the remarks that the house would be on trial, as in the past there had been several convictions for drunkenness and other minor incidents. The brewers E Mason & Co of Maidstone and Caleb Cooper raised the standard of the Imperial, and it still thrives today under the Faversham brewers Shepherd Neame Ltd. Next to the Imperial is the bakery of A Wratten.

Southborough, Sceptre Hill c1965 S152018
The entry into Southborough from Tonbridge down Sceptre Hill has a fine avenue of trees, and a water trough in the centre of the road. Today the hill is often gridlocked with traffic.

Southborough, The Common c1955 S152006
At the top of Sceptre Hill on the way to Tonbridge stands the Hand and Sceptre Hotel; built in 1663, it became an inn in 1728, serving during this time as a district court. The inn was altered in 1897. A ghost of a young girl has been seen going upstairs by several guests over the years. Today we no longer call it by its old name, as the hotel has been converted into a Harvester pub and restaurant. The fountain in the centre of this photograph was erected in 1886 to mark the efforts made by Dr W F Clarke to get Southborough a healthy water supply. On the left is the grocer's shop of H Tranter.

◀ **Southborough
Holden Corner c1955**
S152012
Here we see the pond at
Holden Corner several
years after photograph
No 37896. Fishing still
takes place regularly,
and locals still have to
fight to keep it free from
pollution: last year rats
were seen on the two
islands in the pond, and
action was demanded to
remove them.

◄ Southborough
Holden Corner 1896 37896
A quiet scene at Holden Corner as a gentleman fishes in the pond, watched by a young girl. The pond was often polluted by seepage from a tannery nearby.
In the block of houses facing the pond, H J Chapman was listed as a grocer, carpenter, and undertaker, R Ralph as a chimney sweep and G Singleton as a shopkeeper.

▼ Southborough
Modest Corner 1896 37895
At Modest Corner, some residents held the commoners' right to graze their animals on the common. In the centre of this picture is the Bee Hive public house, which traded from 1873 until 1995; today it is a private dwelling. Other occupations at Modest Corner have been a brewer, a laundry, a cricket ball maker, and a dairyman. Two of the timber-framed buildings are Grade II listed.

◄ Southborough
Modest Corner 1900
44925
A wider view of Modest Corner takes in the large farm with its oast house. At the present time there is a movement to bring back grazing rights by fencing in parts of the common. During the last war, a Red Indian, based nearby with a Canadian regiment, carved some trees on the common with images of his heritage.

Southborough, Bentham Hill from Modest Corner c1955 S152010
On the right of the path heading toward Bentham Hill there is a fine old lamp, plus a telephone pole. At the bottom is the water pumping station, which was built in 1885 and closed in 1973. Note the washing on the line.

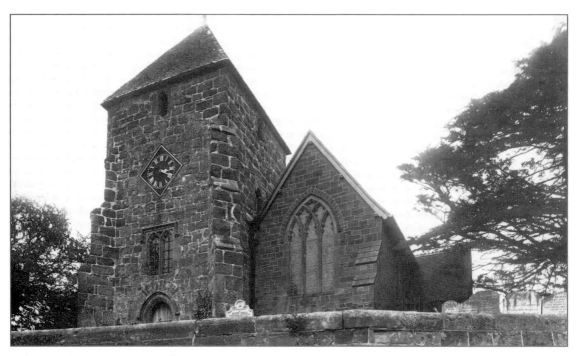

Bidborough, The Church 1896 37903
The church of St Lawrence stands on the hill from which the stone was quarried to build the original building; parts of the church date back to the 10th century. The church was enlarged in 1877 and again in 1894, when it was repaired and an organ installed. The stained windows were the gift of W Chippendale in memory of his wife.

Bidborough
The Hare and Hounds c1965 B87008

The Tunbridge Wells brewers E and H Kelsey built a new pub in the
1870s on the site of an old beerhouse. In 1903 it was described
by the brewers as 'a freehold messuage or tenement and public
house known as the Hare and Hounds situate at Bidborough Kent,
in the occupation of Luke Eade, on a yearly tenancy, at the yearly
rent of £39-10s. Landlord doing outside repairs and insuring'. At
the time, the brewers valued the property at £730-10s. In 1948
Kelseys were taken over by J Greens of Luton, who changed their
name to Flowers in 1954 when the Stratford on Avon brewers
were also taken over. The pub has always been the headquarters
of the Bidborough cricket club.

Penshurst, Rogues Hill 1891 29385 ▶
Going down Rogues Hill towards Penshurst from Bidborough, on the right we have the entrance to Elliotts Farm; the sharp left turn leads to a bridge over the river Medway. Standing tallest among the buildings is the Bridge Tavern, which was run by the Tunbridge Wells brewers E and H Kelsey and described by them in 1903 as 'a copyhold messuage or tenement beerhouse known as the Bridge Tavern with the copyhold cottages and bakehouse adjoining, situate at Penshurst Kent, held of the manor of Penshurst, in the occupation of Charles Henry Colgate on a yearly tenancy, at the yearly rent of £70'. The bakehouse and cottages were demolished for road improvements, and the Bridge Tavern became a private house.

Penshurst

Penshurst, The Village 1891 29387
Coming into the village on the Fordcombe Road, we can see the tower of St John the Baptist's church. The earliest record of a church here was in 1170. St John's is built of stone, chiefly in the late Perpendicular style, and has a tower containing a clock with chimes and 8 bells. It houses a mortuary chapel of the Sidney family, and was restored by Lord De L'Isle and Dudley in 1856

▼ **Penshurst, The Village c1960** P36035

Entering the village from the Leigh Road, on the right we see the Village Hall, built in 1900 at a cost of £4000 by Arnold Hills. It contained a reading room and library, and an entertainment hall seating 300 people, with a stage, a green room, a temperance bar, a billiard room and other rooms. In the centre a car is parked - possibly its passengers are having afternoon tea at the Green Tea Rooms. Note the various building styles in the three buildings ahead.

▼ **Penshurst, The Village 1891** 29388

The building on the left is the Post Office; it has the monogram PSC in its gable ends with ornamental bargeboards. Next to it is Wall Cottage, also with a monogram, DLD this time, and decorative bargeboards and decorative plaster work. This area is known as Leicester Square.

▼ **Penshurst, The Village 1939**
P36013

Another view of Leicester Square. the days before universal car ownership, an advertisement state 'Conveyances go two or three time a week from Tunbridge Wells, wait long enough for visitors to see Penshurst Place, the noble seat of the Sidneys, tickets can be obtaine at the Post Office to view the mansion'. Cyclists, of course, could make the journey too, as the distance is well within an ordinary run. Today the house relies on weddings, film companies, visitors and the many special events that they put on, to help with the enormous cost of running such a large mansion.

◀ **Penshurst Place and the Church 1891** 29393
Penshurst Place is a 14th-century manor house with a fine walled garden, and one of the best baronial halls in the country. It has been the family home of the Sidney family since 1552. In 2002 Philip Sidney, Viscount De L'Isle, unveiled an exciting new family exhibition of portraits, tapestries, furniture and armour to celebrate the continuity of Penshurst Place as a family home for 450 years.

Penshurst, A Cricket Match c1960 P36020
The cricket ground at Penshurst is thought to be one of the oldest in England. In 1728 a Kent side played a Sussex side here for a wager and won by 7 runs. Can there be a better example of English life than a cricket match being played in front of a fine manor house?

Penshurst, The Park 1891 29395
Covering 350 acres, Penshurst Park has many fine oaks; a chancel screen in St John the Baptist's church is made of Penshurst oak. Born at Penshurst Place in 1554, Philip Sidney is known to have planted oaks in the park. One oak is thought to have been here during his time, and is called the Philip Sidney oak. Philip Sidney was a poet and soldier. He entered Parliament in 1581, and was knighted in 1583. In 1585 he was made Governor of Flushing in the Netherlands, and died fighting the Spaniards at Zutphen in 1586.

Tonbridge

Tonbridge
High Street c1950 T101014
We are approaching the High Street from Tonbridge Station.
The library is on the left; it was moved later to Avebury Avenue just round the corner. On
the corner is the tobacconist's shop of A Smith. Across the road is the Angel Hotel, once a
local landmark before its demolition in 1972. Beyond the Angel, the church was also
demolished in 1978. A policeman directs someone toward Avebury Avenue, and the
cyclists enjoy the freedom of the road, unlike today when traffic is often bumper to bumper.

▼ **Tonbridge, The Town Bridge 1951** T101074
A bridge over the river Medway was erected here in 1586. This stone bridge was replaced by an iron bridge of three arches erected on the foundations of the old stone bridge; it was opened in September 1888 and called the Great Bridge, or the Big Bridge. The steps on the left led down to a boat hire quay. Over the bridge is the shop of Gunners, the drapers and furnishers, who were in business for 103 years before their closure in 1984. To the right of Gunners is the National Provincial Bank.

▼ **Tonbridge, Riverside Gardens 1948** T101008
Looking towards the Big Bridge, we can see Riverside Walk and the well-laid-out gardens. On the left is the perimeter wall of Tonbridge Castle.

◀ **Tonbridge, High Street c1905** T1015004
The High Street was very busy with horse transport when this photograph was taken. In the right-hand corner is a drinking trough for animals. The timber-framed 15th-century Chequers Inn was under the control of the Dartford Brewery Company, who had obtained it in 1902 when they took over the Tonbridge brewers W and G Bartram, along with 51 tied houses. A pawnbroker's symbol hangs from the wall next to the Chequers: this belonged to W Peters, who advertised that he wanted 'old false teeth, left off clothes, and old jewellery'. Gunner the cash draper is on the left. An ornate street lamp can also be seen on the left.

◄ **Tonbridge
Ye Old Chequers Inn
c1950** T101037

The Chequers Inn is under
the control of the
Maidstone brewers, Style
and Winch Ltd; they
obtained it in 1924 from the
Dartford Brewery Company.
A fine sign for Sandeman
port and sherry can be seen
on the left. Beyond the
Chequers is the restaurant
of E Aplin, then Achille
Serre Ltd, the dyers, and
then the Westminster Bank.
On the wall of the shop next
to the bank is an
advertisement that reads
'Everything for the baby' -
very apt for Mother and
Baby Ltd, who ran the shop.

◄ **Langton Green
The Village c1960** L324015
On the left of the green at Langton is the church of All Saints, which was erected in 1863. The large white house on the right is Langton House, built by the wealthy Powell family; they owned the green and maintained it for the benefit of the village. Miss Mary Watson, an aunt of the Powells, lived at Langton House, and when she died in 1903 she left money in trust for a church hall. The Village Hall is named the Watson Hall in thanks for her gift. Other residents of Langton House were Charles Cockroft, Prince Fran. Weikershem, and Keith Goodrich.

Langton and Speldhurst

◀ **Langton Green
The Village c1955** L324003
In the centre is the tea shop
known for many years as
Anne's Pantry and run by the
Misses Woolstone and Bulmer.
Later, under the same name,
it was run by R and M Bourne,
then by A and K Tizzard, and
later by J and K Singleton.
Today it is an Indian
restaurant. The same scene
today would reflect the
tremendous increase in motor
traffic - this roadway is one
of the busiest in the area.

◀ **Speldhurst, The Church c1885** 1491
The register for St Mary's church dates
from 1538. The church was destroyed by
fire following a lightning strike on 22
October 1791. St Mary's was rebuilt in
1871 in the Early English style, with only
the base of the old tower used in the new
building. One wonders what the dray is
doing outside the church. Perhaps the
drayman is seeking divine guidance before
descending the steep Speldhurst Hill.

◀ **Frant, The Church and the Village c1955** F173005
The register of St Alban's church dates from 1543, though the building we see here dates from 1822 and was built from plans by J Moutier. It is said that on a clear day you can see Dover, Beachy Head, and Dungeness from the church tower. On the right is the George Hotel, centre of the village's sporting activities. The Bassett family ran the George from 1862 until 1930. One visitor said of the George: 'One is treated with olde-world hospitality and served an excellent real ale'. No man could ask for more.

Frant
and Groombridge

◄ Frant, The Village c1955 F173004
Passing through Frant village on the way to Tunbridge Wells, note the Slow sign in the road: this is to prepare you for the sharp bend by the shops. On the right is the edge of the green, where cricket has been played since at least 1825. The shop on the corner has been a general store, a dried flower shop, and an antique centre.

Groombridge ►
Five Acres c1960 G216016
This Grade II listed building is a 16th-century yeoman's house known as Pollies Hall. It was also known at various times as Killiecrankie and then Five Acres.

◄ **Wadhurst
Lower High Street 190**
49369
Note the early telephone poles on the left. The spire of the Norman church of St Peter and St Paul can be seen above the trees. A horse and cart wait patiently opposite the neatly-fenced houses. Various styles of chimney stacks and a fine finial at the apex of the gabled house set off this peaceful scene.

Wadhurst

◄ **Wadhurst
The Castle 1903** 49376
Once a farmhouse known
as Maplehurst, in 1818 this
property was demolished
to build a house with a
turret at each corner with
castellations, and over
the next few years it was
enlarged. The Castle was
badly damaged by fire in
1933, and the grounds
lost a lot of trees in the
hurricane that hit the
area in October 1987.

◄ **Wadhurst
Wallcrouch 1903** 49357
Between Wadhurst and
Ticehurst is the small hamlet
of Wallcrouch. It had a grocer's
and post office run by
G F Wells, and a shop run by
F M Lloyd. An advertisement
for Mitchell's Prize Crop
Kansas Whiffs cigarettes
appears above the door of
the shop on the left; further
up the road we can see a
postman. A horse and cart
await the owner conducting
business in the store. Today
the building on the right
trades as Inside Out, a garden
ornament premises.

◄ **Lamberhurst
High Street c1955** L323
We are looking along the
High Street as it leads
towards Town Hill. On the
right-hand side we have a
branch of Lloyds Bank, and
beneath the Hovis
advertising sign is Avard and
Son, the bakers. This is
another picture that shows
typical Wealden houses -
timber-framed, weather-
boarded and tile-hung.

Lamberhurst

◄ **Lamberhurst
Hastings Road c1955**

L323010

The busy A21 road goes right
through the village, and the
demand for a bypass is still
ongoing. Note the oast houses
on the right, and four more
behind the weatherboarded
white building, all links with a
time when hop fields were all
around, and oast houses were
needed to dry the hops. Avard
and Co, a Morris garage, is in
the centre of the photograph.

◄ **Lamberhurst
High Street c1955**

L323025

We are entering the
village from Flimwell. On
the right, note the people
waiting for a bus next to
the Village Hall, built in
1921. The Chequers pub
leads to the bridge over
the river Teise; beyond
that is the George and
Dragon pub, which was
rebuilt in 1882 after a fire
destroyed the old inn. On
the left is Avard and Co's
garage; note the different
companies' petrol pumps
and the AA sign.

Lamberhurst, The Chequers c1950 L323021

The Chequers dates from 1412, but an earlier inn was believed to have stood on the site. This photograph was taken when the Maidstone brewers, Fremlins, ran the inn. At that time the landlord was a member of the Beech family, who had connections with the Chequers from 1863 until 1952. In 2000 the inn suffered badly from flooding, and the owner sold it to the Faversham brewers Shepherd Neame Ltd. They invested thousands of pounds in an effort to prevent further flooding.

Lamberhurst, Court Lodge c1955 L323042

Court Lodge was the home of the lord of the manor. This Jacobean building was owned by the Morland family, who had a long-standing connection with the Indian Army; the Lodge held many mementoes of the days of the Raj. Shooting parties were a feature of life at Court Lodge. Local people would join the estate staff for a day of beating, and enjoy the beer and pies supplied.

Hawkhurst

**Hawkhurst
St Laurence's Church 1902** 48258
The earliest reference to the church dates from 1285, and
the building and the bells have been altered over the years.
In August 1944 a German flying bomb fell in the churchyard
and did so much damage that the church was not fully restored
until 1957. The old tree in front of the church died in 1939
and was removed in 1945.

Hawkhurst, Highgate 1904 52116

The house on the left replaced one destroyed by fire in 1890. Next to it is the post office, and in the centre is the spire of All Saints' church, which was consecrated in 1861. To the right is the family grocery store of Farrant & Son. The tall gabled building on the right with the 'Hotel' sign on it was an extension to the Royal Oak, which was built in 1869. An important coaching inn, the Royal Oak was a conversion of three 16th-century cottages. The hotel ran a coach to meet every train that arrived at Hawkhurst station - the coach would have looked like the one we can see in the photograph.

Hawkhurst, Highgate and the Post Office 1925 77043

On the left, with a fine lamp above the entrance, is the General Post Office, Money Order and Telegraph Office, as it used to be known. Could that be telegraph boys outside waiting for a call? The scene is little changed from the other Highgate photograph, 52116, except that we can see the war memorial in front of the Royal Oak.

Hawkhurst
The Colonnade 1902 48245
The colonnade was built in the early 1800s with shops that
included a chemist, a stationer, and a barber's shop. Here we can
see the General Hardware and Implement Store - the barrow
outside was probably used for deliveries. The three boys sitting
on the wall seem fascinated by the photographer.

◀ **Cranbrook, High Street c1925** 77019
Cranbrook has a wealth of old buildings, many dating back to the 16th century, when Cranbrook was the centre of the cloth industry. The buildings on the left remain little changed. Note the canvas canopies and blinds used by the shops, and on the right, the tall telephone pole and short street lamp.

Cranbrook

◄ **Cranbrook**
Stone Street 1902 48234
The first shop on the right was Tye & Sons, who were corn chandlers; next door is Marchant and Tubbs, clothiers and outfitters. A hotel with royal connections takes up the next space: the 15th-century George Hotel had a visit from Queen Elizabeth I in 1573. Over the years the George has served as a court, a prison and as quarters for the military, and still thrives today. Not so lucky was the Bull Hotel in the centre of the photograph - it was demolished in 1936. On the left is the Central Pharmacy, where a horse waits nearby for its cart to be loaded.

◄ **Cranbrook**
The Hill 1913 65426
This photograph contains some of the best examples of Wealden buildings; some are timber-framed, some weatherboarded, and some faced with stucco. The mill can be seen behind the houses. The tall building with the bay windows was once the Crane coffee tavern.

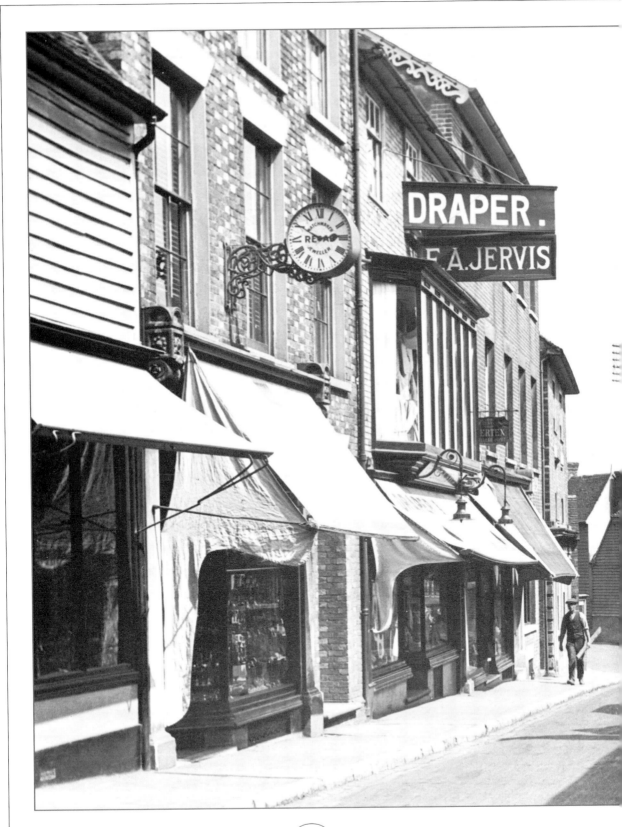

**Cranbrook
Stone Street 1925**
77023
The Union Mill, built in
1814, can be seen in
the centre; at 21m high,
it is the largest smock
mill in the country. It
was taken over in 1960
by Kent County Council
and put into good
repair. The Cranbrook
Windmill Association
was formed in 1982 to
look after the mill, and
corn is ground to
produce flour which is
sold at the mill. Also in
the scene is a milkman
with a churn attached to
his bike. A large clock
hangs on the wall next
to E A Jervis, the draper
and outfitter, who has
two ornate lamps
hanging outside his
shop.

◀ **Horsmonden
The Green 1903** 50551
Looking across the green,
on the right-hand side we
can see the boot and
shoe shop of the Foord
family, and in the centre
the butcher's shop of
H J Harvey. On the left-hand
side is the Institute and
Reading Room built by
J Austin; the turret and clock
were added in 1887 as a
memorial of the Jubilee of
Queen Victoria.

Horsmonden

◀ **Horsmonden**
The Old Walnut Tree
1901 46401
The old walnut tree
stood near St Margaret's
church, and was so big
that it required props to
hold it up and keep the
roadway clear. It died
some years ago.

◀ **Horsmonden**
The Village 1925 77039
The village green was
known as the heath, and
on the left we can see
the Heath Engineering
Works. In the centre is
the Institute, and the
shop with the blind
down was F Bromley, a
butcher's. It is said that a
ghost of a highwayman
known as 'Bill the Buck',
who was hung and
gibbeted at
Horsmonden, walks
across the green.

Horsmonden, The Village 1925 77040

On the road toward Goudhurst, we have on the right the shop of F Peters, a grocer. In the centre is the Gun public house; it takes its name from the local iron and smelting works that flourished in the area where guns were cast for Charles I, Cromwell, and the navy. Parts of the pub date back to 1560, and it was first licensed in 1570. At the time of the photograph it was selling Westerham ales, the trade name of Bushell Watkins & Smith Ltd. On the left is W Crowhurst's shop, known as the Bazaar.

Horsmonden, The Village 1903 50550

Heading toward the village and Brenchley, with the Gun at the top of the hill, on the right-hand side we have a pond with railings and a water trough in front. On the left is a pile of rubble close to the stables of the Gun. Note the different size and shape of the chimneys, and the lines of washing in the gardens.

Index

Frith Book Co Titles

www.francisfrith.co.uk

The Frith Book Company publishes over 100 new titles each year. A selection of those currently available are listed below. For latest catalogue please contact Frith Book Co.

Town Books 96 pages, approx 100 photos. County and Themed Books 128 pages, approx 150 photos (unless specified). All titles hardback laminated case and jacket except those indicated pb (paperback)

Title	ISBN	Price	Title	ISBN	Price
Amersham, Chesham & Rickmansworth (pb)	1-85937-340-2	£9.99	Derby (pb)	1-85937-367-4	£9.99
Ancient Monuments & Stone Circles	1-85937-143-4	£17.99	Derbyshire (pb)	1-85937-196-5	£9.99
Aylesbury (pb)	1-85937-227-9	£9.99	Devon (pb)	1-85937-297-x	£9.99
Bakewell	1-85937-113-2	£12.99	Dorset (pb)	1-85937-269-4	£9.99
Barnstaple (pb)	1-85937-300-3	£9.99	Dorset Churches	1-85937-172-8	£17.99
Bath (pb)	1-85937419-0	£9.99	Dorset Coast (pb)	1-85937-299-6	£9.99
Bedford (pb)	1-85937-205-8	£9.99	Dorset Living Memories	1-85937-210-4	£14.99
Berkshire (pb)	1-85937-191-4	£9.99	Down the Severn	1-85937-118-3	£14.99
Berkshire Churches	1-85937-170-1	£17.99	Down the Thames (pb)	1-85937-278-3	£9.99
Blackpool (pb)	1-85937-382-8	£9.99	Down the Trent	1-85937-311-9	£14.99
Bognor Regis (pb)	1-85937-431-x	£9.99	Dublin (pb)	1-85937-231-7	£9.99
Bournemouth	1-85937-067-5	£12.99	East Anglia (pb)	1-85937-265-1	£9.99
Bradford (pb)	1-85937-204-x	£9.99	East London	1-85937-080-2	£14.99
Brighton & Hove(pb)	1-85937-192-2	£8.99	East Sussex	1-85937-130-2	£14.99
Bristol (pb)	1-85937-264-3	£9.99	Eastbourne	1-85937-061-6	£12.99
British Life A Century Ago (pb)	1-85937-213-9	£9.99	Edinburgh (pb)	1-85937-193-0	£8.99
Buckinghamshire (pb)	1-85937-200-7	£9.99	England in the 1880s	1-85937-331-3	£17.99
Camberley (pb)	1-85937-222-8	£9.99	English Castles (pb)	1-85937-434-4	£9.99
Cambridge (pb)	1-85937-422-0	£9.99	English Country Houses	1-85937-161-2	£17.99
Cambridgeshire (pb)	1-85937-420-4	£9.99	Essex (pb)	1-85937-270-8	£9.99
Canals & Waterways (pb)	1-85937-291-0	£9.99	Exeter	1-85937-126-4	£12.99
Canterbury Cathedral (pb)	1-85937-179-5	£9.99	Exmoor	1-85937-132-9	£14.99
Cardiff (pb)	1-85937-093-4	£9.99	Falmouth	1-85937-066-7	£12.99
Carmarthenshire	1-85937-216-3	£14.99	Folkestone (pb)	1-85937-124-8	£9.99
Chelmsford (pb)	1-85937-310-0	£9.99	Glasgow (pb)	1-85937-190-6	£9.99
Cheltenham (pb)	1-85937-095-0	£9.99	Gloucestershire	1-85937-102-7	£14.99
Cheshire (pb)	1-85937-271-6	£9.99	Great Yarmouth (pb)	1-85937-426-3	£9.99
Chester	1-85937-090-x	£12.99	Greater Manchester (pb)	1-85937-266-x	£9.99
Chesterfield	1-85937-378-x	£9.99	Guildford (pb)	1-85937-410-7	£9.99
Chichester (pb)	1-85937-228-7	£9.99	Hampshire (pb)	1-85937-279-1	£9.99
Colchester (pb)	1-85937-188-4	£8.99	Hampshire Churches (pb)	1-85937-207-4	£9.99
Cornish Coast	1-85937-163-9	£14.99	Harrogate	1-85937-423-9	£9.99
Cornwall (pb)	1-85937-229-5	£9.99	Hastings & Bexhill (pb)	1-85937-131-0	£9.99
Cornwall Living Memories	1-85937-248-1	£14.99	Heart of Lancashire (pb)	1-85937-197-3	£9.99
Cotswolds (pb)	1-85937-230-9	£9.99	Helston (pb)	1-85937-214-7	£9.99
Cotswolds Living Memories	1-85937-255-4	£14.99	Hereford (pb)	1-85937-175-2	£9.99
County Durham	1-85937-123-x	£14.99	Herefordshire	1-85937-174-4	£14.99
Croydon Living Memories	1-85937-162-0	£9.99	Hertfordshire (pb)	1-85937-247-3	£9.99
Cumbria	1-85937-101-9	£14.99	Horsham (pb)	1-85937-432-8	£9.99
Dartmoor	1-85937-145-0	£14.99	Humberside	1-85937-215-5	£14.99
			Hythe, Romney Marsh & Ashford	1-85937-256-2	£9.99

Available from your local bookshop or from the publisher

Frith Book Co Titles (continued)

Title	ISBN	Price	Title	ISBN	Price
Ipswich (pb)	1-85937-424-7	£9.99	St Ives (pb)	1-85937415-8	£9.99
Ireland (pb)	1-85937-181-7	£9.99	Scotland (pb)	1-85937-182-5	£9.99
Isle of Man (pb)	1-85937-268-6	£9.99	Scottish Castles (pb)	1-85937-323-2	£9.99
Isles of Scilly	1-85937-136-1	£14.99	Sevenoaks & Tunbridge	1-85937-057-8	£12.99
Isle of Wight (pb)	1-85937-429-8	£9.99	Sheffield, South Yorks (pb)	1-85937-267-8	£9.99
Isle of Wight Living Memories	1-85937-304-6	£14.99	Shrewsbury (pb)	1-85937-325-9	£9.99
Kent (pb)	1-85937-189-2	£9.99	Shropshire (pb)	1-85937-326-7	£9.99
Kent Living Memories	1-85937-125-6	£14.99	Somerset	1-85937-153-1	£14.99
Lake District (pb)	1-85937-275-9	£9.99	South Devon Coast	1-85937-107-8	£14.99
Lancaster, Morecambe & Heysham (pb)	1-85937-233-3	£9.99	South Devon Living Memories	1-85937-168-x	£14.99
Leeds (pb)	1-85937-202-3	£9.99	South Hams	1-85937-220-1	£14.99
Leicester	1-85937-073-x	£12.99	Southampton (pb)	1-85937-427-1	£9.99
Leicestershire (pb)	1-85937-185-x	£9.99	Southport (pb)	1-85937-425-5	£9.99
Lincolnshire (pb)	1-85937-433-6	£9.99	Staffordshire	1-85937-047-0	£12.99
Liverpool & Merseyside (pb)	1-85937-234-1	£9.99	Stratford upon Avon	1-85937-098-5	£12.99
London (pb)	1-85937-183-3	£9.99	Suffolk (pb)	1-85937-221-x	£9.99
Ludlow (pb)	1-85937-176-0	£9.99	Suffolk Coast	1-85937-259-7	£14.99
Luton (pb)	1-85937-235-x	£9.99	Surrey (pb)	1-85937-240-6	£9.99
Maidstone	1-85937-056-x	£14.99	Sussex (pb)	1-85937-184-1	£9.99
Manchester (pb)	1-85937-198-1	£9.99	Swansea (pb)	1-85937-167-1	£9.99
Middlesex	1-85937-158-2	£14.99	Tees Valley & Cleveland	1-85937-211-2	£14.99
New Forest	1-85937-128-0	£14.99	Thanet (pb)	1-85937-116-7	£9.99
Newark (pb)	1-85937-366-6	£9.99	Tiverton (pb)	1-85937-178-7	£9.99
Newport, Wales (pb)	1-85937-258-9	£9.99	Torbay	1-85937-063-2	£12.99
Newquay (pb)	1-85937-421-2	£9.99	Truro	1-85937-147-7	£12.99
Norfolk (pb)	1-85937-195-7	£9.99	Victorian and Edwardian Cornwall	1-85937-252-x	£14.99
Norfolk Living Memories	1-85937-217-1	£14.99	Victorian & Edwardian Devon	1-85937-253-8	£14.99
Northamptonshire	1-85937-150-7	£14.99	Victorian & Edwardian Kent	1-85937-149-3	£14.99
Northumberland Tyne & Wear (pb)	1-85937-281-3	£9.99	Vic & Ed Maritime Album	1-85937-144-2	£17.99
North Devon Coast	1-85937-146-9	£14.99	Victorian and Edwardian Sussex	1-85937-157-4	£14.99
North Devon Living Memories	1-85937-261-9	£14.99	Victorian & Edwardian Yorkshire	1-85937-154-x	£14.99
North London	1-85937-206-6	£14.99	Victorian Seaside	1-85937-159-0	£17.99
North Wales (pb)	1-85937-298-8	£9.99	Villages of Devon (pb)	1-85937-293-7	£9.99
North Yorkshire (pb)	1-85937-236-8	£9.99	Villages of Kent (pb)	1-85937-294-5	£9.99
Norwich (pb)	1-85937-194-9	£8.99	Villages of Sussex (pb)	1-85937-295-3	£9.99
Nottingham (pb)	1-85937-324-0	£9.99	Warwickshire (pb)	1-85937-203-1	£9.99
Nottinghamshire (pb)	1-85937-187-6	£9.99	Welsh Castles (pb)	1-85937-322-4	£9.99
Oxford (pb)	1-85937-411-5	£9.99	West Midlands (pb)	1-85937-289-9	£9.99
Oxfordshire (pb)	1-85937-430-1	£9.99	West Sussex	1-85937-148-5	£14.99
Peak District (pb)	1-85937-280-5	£9.99	West Yorkshire (pb)	1-85937-201-5	£9.99
Penzance	1-85937-069-1	£12.99	Weymouth (pb)	1-85937-209-0	£9.99
Peterborough (pb)	1-85937-219-8	£9.99	Wiltshire (pb)	1-85937-277-5	£9.99
Piers	1-85937-237-6	£17.99	Wiltshire Churches (pb)	1-85937-171-x	£9.99
Plymouth	1-85937-119-1	£12.99	Wiltshire Living Memories	1-85937-245-7	£14.99
Poole & Sandbanks (pb)	1-85937-251-1	£9.99	Winchester (pb)	1-85937-428-x	£9.99
Preston (pb)	1-85937-212-0	£9.99	Windmills & Watermills	1-85937-242-2	£17.99
Reading (pb)	1-85937-238-4	£9.99	Worcester (pb)	1-85937-165-5	£9.99
Romford (pb)	1-85937-319-4	£9.99	Worcestershire	1-85937-152-3	£14.99
Salisbury (pb)	1-85937-239-2	£9.99	York (pb)	1-85937-199-x	£9.99
Scarborough (pb)	1-85937-379-8	£9.99	Yorkshire (pb)	1-85937-186-8	£9.99
St Albans (pb)	1-85937-341-0	£9.99	Yorkshire Living Memories	1-85937-166-3	£14.99

See Frith books on the internet www.francisfrith.co.uk

FRITH PRODUCTS & SERVICES

Francis Frith would doubtless be pleased to know that the pioneering publishing venture he started in 1860 still continues today. A hundred and forty years later, The Francis Frith Collection continues in the same innovative tradition and is now one of the foremost publishers of vintage photographs in the world. Some of the current activities include:

Interior Decoration

Today Frith's photographs can be seen framed and as giant wall murals in thousands of pubs, restaurants, hotels, banks, retail stores and other public buildings throughout the country. In every case they enhance the unique local atmosphere of the places they depict and provide reminders of gentler days in an increasingly busy and frenetic world.

Product Promotions

Frith products are used by many major companies to promote the sales of their own products or to reinforce their own history and heritage. Frith promotions have been used by Hovis bread, Courage beers, Scots Porage Oats, Colman's mustard, Cadbury's foods, Mellow Birds coffee, Dunhill pipe tobacco, Guinness, and Bulmer's Cider.

Genealogy and Family History

As the interest in family history and roots grows world-wide, more and more people are turning to Frith's photographs of Great Britain for images of the towns, villages and streets where their ancestors lived; and, of course, photographs of the churches and chapels where their ancestors were christened, married and buried are an essential part of every genealogy tree and family album.

Frith Products

All Frith photographs are available Framed or just as Mounted Prints and Posters (size 23 x 16 inches). These may be ordered from the address below. From time to time other products - Address Books, Calendars, Table Mats, etc - are available.

The Internet

Already twenty thousand Frith photographs can be viewed and purchased on the internet through the Frith websites and a myriad of partner sites.

For more detailed information on Frith companies and products, look at these sites:

www.francisfrith.co.uk
www.francisfrith.com
(for North American visitors)

See the complete list of Frith Books at:

www.francisfrith.co.uk

This web site is regularly updated with the latest list of publications from the Frith Book Company. If you wish to buy books relating to another part of the country that your local bookshop does not stock, you may purchase on-line.

For further information, trade, or author enquiries please contact us at the address below:
The Francis Frith Collection, Frith's Barn, Teffont, Salisbury, Wiltshire, England SP3 5QP.
Tel: +44 (0)1722 716 376 Fax: +44 (0)1722 716 881 Email: sales@francisfrith.co.uk

See Frith books on the internet www.francisfrith.co.uk